CW00521022

👤 _____

🏠 _____

_____

☎ _____

_____

✉ _____

2023

JANUARY

MO	TU	WE	TH	FR	SA	SU
						1
2	3	4	5	6	7	8
9	10	11	12	13	14	15
16	17	18	19	20	21	22
23	24	25	26	27	28	29
30	31					

FEBRUARY

MO	TU	WE	TH	FR	SA	SU
		1	2	3	4	5
6	7	8	9	10	11	12
13	14	15	16	17	18	19
20	21	22	23	24	25	26
27	28					

MARCH

MO	TU	WE	TH	FR	SA	SU
		1	2	3	4	5
6	7	8	9	10	11	12
13	14	15	16	17	18	19
20	21	22	23	24	25	26
27	28	29	30	31		

APRIL

MO	TU	WE	TH	FR	SA	SU
					1	2
3	4	5	6	7	8	9
10	11	12	13	14	15	16
17	18	19	20	21	22	23
24	25	26	27	28	29	30

MAY

MO	TU	WE	TH	FR	SA	SU
1	2	3	4	5	6	7
8	9	10	11	12	13	14
15	16	17	18	19	20	21
22	23	24	25	26	27	28
29	30	31				

JUNE

MO	TU	WE	TH	FR	SA	SU
			1	2	3	4
5	6	7	8	9	10	11
12	13	14	15	16	17	18
19	20	21	22	23	24	25
26	27	28	29	30		

JULY

MO	TU	WE	TH	FR	SA	SU
					1	2
3	4	5	6	7	8	9
10	11	12	13	14	15	16
17	18	19	20	21	22	23
24	25	26	27	28	29	30
31						

AUGUST

MO	TU	WE	TH	FR	SA	SU
	1	2	3	4	5	6
7	8	9	10	11	12	13
14	15	16	17	18	19	20
21	22	23	24	25	26	27
28	29	30	31			

SEPTEMBER

MO	TU	WE	TH	FR	SA	SU
				1	2	3
4	5	6	7	8	9	10
11	12	13	14	15	16	17
18	19	20	21	22	23	24
25	26	27	28	29	30	

OCTOBER

MO	TU	WE	TH	FR	SA	SU
						1
2	3	4	5	6	7	8
9	10	11	12	13	14	15
16	17	18	19	20	21	22
23	24	25	26	27	28	29
30	31					

NOVEMBER

MO	TU	WE	TH	FR	SA	SU
		1	2	3	4	5
6	7	8	9	10	11	12
13	14	15	16	17	18	19
20	21	22	23	24	25	26
27	28	29	30			

DECEMBER

MO	TU	WE	TH	FR	SA	SU
				1	2	3
4	5	6	7	8	9	10
11	12	13	14	15	16	17
18	19	20	21	22	23	24
25	26	27	28	29	30	31

2024

JANUARY

MO	TU	WE	TH	FR	SA	SU
1	2	3	4	5	6	7
8	9	10	11	12	13	14
15	16	17	18	19	20	21
22	23	24	25	26	27	28
29	30	31				

FEBRUARY

MO	TU	WE	TH	FR	SA	SU
			1	2	3	4
5	6	7	8	9	10	11
12	13	14	15	16	17	18
19	20	21	22	23	24	25
26	27	28	29			

MARCH

MO	TU	WE	TH	FR	SA	SU
				1	2	3
4	5	6	7	8	9	10
11	12	13	14	15	16	17
18	19	20	21	22	23	24
25	26	27	28	29	30	31

APRIL

MO	TU	WE	TH	FR	SA	SU
1	2	3	4	5	6	7
8	9	10	11	12	13	14
15	16	17	18	19	20	21
22	23	24	25	26	27	28
29	30					

MAY

MO	TU	WE	TH	FR	SA	SU
		1	2	3	4	5
6	7	8	9	10	11	12
13	14	15	16	17	18	19
20	21	22	23	24	25	26
27	28	29	30	31		

JUNE

MO	TU	WE	TH	FR	SA	SU
					1	2
3	4	5	6	7	8	9
10	11	12	13	14	15	16
17	18	19	20	21	22	23
24	25	26	27	28	29	30

JULY

MO	TU	WE	TH	FR	SA	SU
1	2	3	4	5	6	7
8	9	10	11	12	13	14
15	16	17	18	19	20	21
22	23	24	25	26	27	28
29	30	31				

AUGUST

MO	TU	WE	TH	FR	SA	SU
			1	2	3	4
5	6	7	8	9	10	11
12	13	14	15	16	17	18
19	20	21	22	23	24	25
26	27	28	29	30	31	

SEPTEMBER

MO	TU	WE	TH	FR	SA	SU
						1
2	3	4	5	6	7	8
9	10	11	12	13	14	15
16	17	18	19	20	21	22
23	24	25	26	27	28	29
30						

OCTOBER

MO	TU	WE	TH	FR	SA	SU
	1	2	3	4	5	6
7	8	9	10	11	12	13
14	15	16	17	18	19	20
21	22	23	24	25	26	27
28	29	30	31			

NOVEMBER

MO	TU	WE	TH	FR	SA	SU
				1	2	3
4	5	6	7	8	9	10
11	12	13	14	15	16	17
18	19	20	21	22	23	24
25	26	27	28	29	30	

DECEMBER

MO	TU	WE	TH	FR	SA	SU
						1
2	3	4	5	6	7	8
9	10	11	12	13	14	15
16	17	18	19	20	21	22
23	24	25	26	27	28	29
30	31					

CUSTOMER NAME	PHONE NUMBER	CUSTOMER NAME	PHONE NUMBER

CUSTOMER NAME	PHONE NUMBER	CUSTOMER NAME	PHONE NUMBER

TIME		SERVICE	CUSTOMER

DAY

MONTH ....

YEAR ....

TO DO LIST			
8 AM	00		
	30		
9 AM	00		
	30		
10 AM	00		
	30		
11 AM	00		
	30		
12 PM	00		
MATERIALS LIST	30		
1 PM	00		
	30		
2 PM	00		
	30		
3 PM	00		
	30		
QUOTES			
4 PM	00		
	30		
5 PM	00		
	30		
6 PM	00		
	30		
7 PM	00		
	30		
8 PM	00		
	30		

SCHEDULE ▼ APPOINTMENTS ▼ PLANNER

DAY	TIME		SERVICE	CUSTOMER
MONTH .... **YEAR**	**8** AM	00		
		30		
TO DO LIST	**9** AM	00		
		30		
	10 AM	00		
		30		
	11 AM	00		
		30		
	12 PM	00		
MATERIALS LIST		30		
	1 PM	00		
		30		
	2 PM	00		
		30		
	3 PM	00		
		30		
QUOTES	**4** PM	00		
		30		
	5 PM	00		
		30		
	6 PM	00		
		30		
	7 PM	00		
		30		
	8 PM	00		
		30		

DAY	TIME		SERVICE	CUSTOMER
MONTH .... **YEAR**	**8** AM	00		
		30		
TO DO LIST	**9** AM	00		
		30		
	10 AM	00		
		30		
	11 AM	00		
		30		
	12 PM	00		
MATERIALS LIST		30		
	1 PM	00		
		30		
	2 PM	00		
		30		
	3 PM	00		
		30		
QUOTES	**4** PM	00		
		30		
	5 PM	00		
		30		
	6 PM	00		
		30		
	7 PM	00		
		30		
	8 PM	00		
		30		

DAY	TIME		SERVICE	CUSTOMER
MONTH .... **YEAR**	8 AM	00		
		30		
TO DO LIST	9 AM	00		
		30		
	10 AM	00		
		30		
	11 AM	00		
		30		
	12 PM	00		
MATERIALS LIST		30		
	1 PM	00		
		30		
	2 PM	00		
		30		
	3 PM	00		
		30		
QUOTES	4 PM	00		
		30		
	5 PM	00		
		30		
	6 PM	00		
		30		
	7 PM	00		
		30		
	8 PM	00		
		30		

DAY	TIME		SERVICE	CUSTOMER
MONTH .... **YEAR**	**8** AM	00		
		30		
TO DO LIST	**9** AM	00		
		30		
	10 AM	00		
		30		
	11 AM	00		
		30		
	12 PM	00		
MATERIALS LIST		30		
	1 PM	00		
		30		
	2 PM	00		
		30		
	3 PM	00		
		30		
QUOTES	**4** PM	00		
		30		
	5 PM	00		
		30		
	6 PM	00		
		30		
	7 PM	00		
		30		
	8 PM	00		
		30		

DAY		TIME		SERVICE	CUSTOMER
MONTH .... **YEAR**		**8** AM	00		
			30		
TO DO LIST		**9** AM	00		
			30		
		10 AM	00		
			30		
		11 AM	00		
			30		
		12 PM	00		
MATERIALS LIST			30		
		1 PM	00		
			30		
		2 PM	00		
			30		
		3 PM	00		
			30		
QUOTES		**4** PM	00		
			30		
		5 PM	00		
			30		
		6 PM	00		
			30		
		7 PM	00		
			30		
		8 PM	00		
			30		

DAY	TIME		SERVICE	CUSTOMER
DAY MONTH .... YEAR	8 AM	00		
		30		
TO DO LIST	9 AM	00		
		30		
	10 AM	00		
		30		
	11 AM	00		
		30		
	12 PM	00		
MATERIALS LIST		30		
	1 PM	00		
		30		
	2 PM	00		
		30		
	3 PM	00		
		30		
QUOTES	4 PM	00		
		30		
	5 PM	00		
		30		
	6 PM	00		
		30		
	7 PM	00		
		30		
	8 PM	00		
		30		

DAY	TIME		SERVICE	CUSTOMER
MONTH .... **YEAR**	8 AM	00		
		30		
TO DO LIST	9 AM	00		
		30		
	10 AM	00		
		30		
	11 AM	00		
		30		
	12 PM	00		
MATERIALS LIST		30		
	1 PM	00		
		30		
	2 PM	00		
		30		
	3 PM	00		
		30		
QUOTES	4 PM	00		
		30		
	5 PM	00		
		30		
	6 PM	00		
		30		
	7 PM	00		
		30		
	8 PM	00		
		30		

DAY	TIME		SERVICE	CUSTOMER
MONTH .... **YEAR**	**8** AM	00		
		30		
TO DO LIST	**9** AM	00		
		30		
	10 AM	00		
		30		
	11 AM	00		
		30		
	12 PM	00		
MATERIALS LIST		30		
	1 PM	00		
		30		
	2 PM	00		
		30		
	3 PM	00		
		30		
QUOTES	**4** PM	00		
		30		
	5 PM	00		
		30		
	6 PM	00		
		30		
	7 PM	00		
		30		
	8 PM	00		
		30		

DAY	TIME		SERVICE	CUSTOMER
MONTH .... **YEAR**	**8** AM	00		
		30		
TO DO LIST	**9** AM	00		
		30		
	10 AM	00		
		30		
	11 AM	00		
		30		
	12 PM	00		
MATERIALS LIST		30		
	1 PM	00		
		30		
	2 PM	00		
		30		
	3 PM	00		
		30		
QUOTES	**4** PM	00		
		30		
	5 PM	00		
		30		
	6 PM	00		
		30		
	7 PM	00		
		30		
	8 PM	00		
		30		

DAY		TIME		SERVICE	CUSTOMER
MONTH		**8** AM	00		
YEAR			30		
TO DO LIST		**9** AM	00		
			30		
		10 AM	00		
			30		
		11 AM	00		
			30		
		12 PM	00		
MATERIALS LIST			30		
		1 PM	00		
			30		
		2 PM	00		
			30		
		3 PM	00		
			30		
QUOTES		**4** PM	00		
			30		
		5 PM	00		
			30		
		6 PM	00		
			30		
		7 PM	00		
			30		
		8 PM	00		
			30		

		TIME		SERVICE	CUSTOMER
DAY		**8** AM	00		
MONTH			30		
YEAR		**9** AM	00		
TO DO LIST			30		
		10 AM	00		
			30		
		11 AM	00		
			30		
		12 PM	00		
MATERIALS LIST			30		
		1 PM	00		
			30		
		2 PM	00		
			30		
		3 PM	00		
			30		
QUOTES		**4** PM	00		
			30		
		5 PM	00		
			30		
		6 PM	00		
			30		
		7 PM	00		
			30		
		8 PM	00		
			30		

DAY	TIME		SERVICE	CUSTOMER
MONTH .... YEAR	8 AM	00		
		30		
TO DO LIST	9 AM	00		
		30		
	10 AM	00		
		30		
	11 AM	00		
		30		
	12 PM	00		
MATERIALS LIST		30		
	1 PM	00		
		30		
	2 PM	00		
		30		
	3 PM	00		
		30		
QUOTES	4 PM	00		
		30		
	5 PM	00		
		30		
	6 PM	00		
		30		
	7 PM	00		
		30		
	8 PM	00		
		30		

DAY	TIME		SERVICE	CUSTOMER
MONTH .... **YEAR**	8 AM	00		
		30		
TO DO LIST	9 AM	00		
		30		
	10 AM	00		
		30		
	11 AM	00		
		30		
	12 PM	00		
MATERIALS LIST		30		
	1 PM	00		
		30		
	2 PM	00		
		30		
	3 PM	00		
		30		
QUOTES	4 PM	00		
		30		
	5 PM	00		
		30		
	6 PM	00		
		30		
	7 PM	00		
		30		
	8 PM	00		
		30		

SCHEDULE ▼ APPOINTMENTS ▼ PLANNER

DAY	TIME		SERVICE	CUSTOMER
MONTH	8 AM	00		
YEAR		30		
TO DO LIST	9 AM	00		
		30		
	10 AM	00		
		30		
	11 AM	00		
		30		
	12 PM	00		
MATERIALS LIST		30		
	1 PM	00		
		30		
	2 PM	00		
		30		
	3 PM	00		
		30		
QUOTES	4 PM	00		
		30		
	5 PM	00		
		30		
	6 PM	00		
		30		
	7 PM	00		
		30		
	8 PM	00		
		30		

DAY	TIME		SERVICE	CUSTOMER
MONTH .... **YEAR**	8 AM	00		
		30		
TO DO LIST	9 AM	00		
		30		
	10 AM	00		
		30		
	11 AM	00		
		30		
	12 PM	00		
MATERIALS LIST		30		
	1 PM	00		
		30		
	2 PM	00		
		30		
	3 PM	00		
		30		
QUOTES	4 PM	00		
		30		
	5 PM	00		
		30		
	6 PM	00		
		30		
	7 PM	00		
		30		
	8 PM	00		
		30		

DAY	TIME		SERVICE	CUSTOMER
MONTH .... **YEAR**	**8** AM	00		
		30		
TO DO LIST	**9** AM	00		
		30		
	10 AM	00		
		30		
	11 AM	00		
		30		
	12 PM	00		
MATERIALS LIST		30		
	1 PM	00		
		30		
	2 PM	00		
		30		
	3 PM	00		
		30		
QUOTES	**4** PM	00		
		30		
	5 PM	00		
		30		
	6 PM	00		
		30		
	7 PM	00		
		30		
	8 PM	00		
		30		

DAY	TIME		SERVICE	CUSTOMER
MONTH .... **YEAR**	8 AM	00		
		30		
TO DO LIST	9 AM	00		
		30		
	10 AM	00		
		30		
	11 AM	00		
		30		
	12 PM	00		
MATERIALS LIST		30		
	1 PM	00		
		30		
	2 PM	00		
		30		
	3 PM	00		
		30		
QUOTES	4 PM	00		
		30		
	5 PM	00		
		30		
	6 PM	00		
		30		
	7 PM	00		
		30		
	8 PM	00		
		30		

DAY	TIME		SERVICE	CUSTOMER
MONTH .... **YEAR**	8 AM	00		
		30		
TO DO LIST	9 AM	00		
		30		
	10 AM	00		
		30		
	11 AM	00		
		30		
	12 PM	00		
MATERIALS LIST		30		
	1 PM	00		
		30		
	2 PM	00		
		30		
	3 PM	00		
		30		
QUOTES	4 PM	00		
		30		
	5 PM	00		
		30		
	6 PM	00		
		30		
	7 PM	00		
		30		
	8 PM	00		
		30		

	TIME		SERVICE	CUSTOMER
DAY .... **MONTH** .... **YEAR**	**8** AM	**00**		
		30		
TO DO LIST	**9** AM	**00**		
		30		
	10 AM	**00**		
		30		
	11 AM	**00**		
		30		
	12 PM	**00**		
MATERIALS LIST		**30**		
	1 PM	**00**		
		30		
	2 PM	**00**		
		30		
	3 PM	**00**		
		30		
QUOTES	**4** PM	**00**		
		30		
	5 PM	**00**		
		30		
	6 PM	**00**		
		30		
	7 PM	**00**		
		30		
	8 PM	**00**		
		30		

DAY	TIME		SERVICE	CUSTOMER
MONTH .... **YEAR**	8 AM	00		
		30		
TO DO LIST	9 AM	00		
		30		
	10 AM	00		
		30		
	11 AM	00		
		30		
	12 PM	00		
MATERIALS LIST		30		
	1 PM	00		
		30		
	2 PM	00		
		30		
	3 PM	00		
		30		
QUOTES	4 PM	00		
		30		
	5 PM	00		
		30		
	6 PM	00		
		30		
	7 PM	00		
		30		
	8 PM	00		
		30		

DAY	TIME		SERVICE	CUSTOMER
MONTH .... **YEAR**	**8** AM	00		
		30		
TO DO LIST	**9** AM	00		
		30		
	10 AM	00		
		30		
	11 AM	00		
		30		
	12 PM	00		
MATERIALS LIST		30		
	1 PM	00		
		30		
	2 PM	00		
		30		
	3 PM	00		
		30		
QUOTES	**4** PM	00		
		30		
	5 PM	00		
		30		
	6 PM	00		
		30		
	7 PM	00		
		30		
	8 PM	00		
		30		

DAY		TIME		SERVICE	CUSTOMER
MONTH	....	**8** AM	00		
YEAR	....		30		
TO DO LIST		**9** AM	00		
			30		
		10 AM	00		
			30		
		11 AM	00		
			30		
		12 PM	00		
MATERIALS LIST			30		
		1 PM	00		
			30		
		2 PM	00		
			30		
		3 PM	00		
			30		
QUOTES		**4** PM	00		
			30		
		5 PM	00		
			30		
		6 PM	00		
			30		
		7 PM	00		
			30		
		8 PM	00		
			30		

DAY	TIME		SERVICE	CUSTOMER
MONTH .... **YEAR**	**8** AM	00		
		30		
TO DO LIST	**9** AM	00		
		30		
	10 AM	00		
		30		
	11 AM	00		
		30		
	12 PM	00		
MATERIALS LIST		30		
	1 PM	00		
		30		
	2 PM	00		
		30		
	3 PM	00		
		30		
QUOTES	**4** PM	00		
		30		
	5 PM	00		
		30		
	6 PM	00		
		30		
	7 PM	00		
		30		
	8 PM	00		
		30		

DAY		TIME		SERVICE	CUSTOMER
MONTH		**8** AM	00		
YEAR			30		
TO DO LIST		**9** AM	00		
			30		
		10 AM	00		
			30		
		11 AM	00		
			30		
		12 PM	00		
MATERIALS LIST			30		
		1 PM	00		
			30		
		2 PM	00		
			30		
		3 PM	00		
			30		
QUOTES		**4** PM	00		
			30		
		5 PM	00		
			30		
		6 PM	00		
			30		
		7 PM	00		
			30		
		8 PM	00		
			30		

DAY		TIME		SERVICE	CUSTOMER
MONTH		**8** AM	00		
YEAR			30		
TO DO LIST		**9** AM	00		
			30		
		10 AM	00		
			30		
		11 AM	00		
			30		
		12 PM	00		
MATERIALS LIST			30		
		1 PM	00		
			30		
		2 PM	00		
			30		
		3 PM	00		
			30		
QUOTES		**4** PM	00		
			30		
		5 PM	00		
			30		
		6 PM	00		
			30		
		7 PM	00		
			30		
		8 PM	00		
			30		

DAY					

	TIME		SERVICE	CUSTOMER
DAY MONTH YEAR	**8** AM	00		
		30		
TO DO LIST	**9** AM	00		
		30		
	10 AM	00		
		30		
	11 AM	00		
		30		
	12 PM	00		
MATERIALS LIST		30		
	1 PM	00		
		30		
	2 PM	00		
		30		
	3 PM	00		
		30		
QUOTES	**4** PM	00		
		30		
	5 PM	00		
		30		
	6 PM	00		
		30		
	7 PM	00		
		30		
	8 PM	00		
		30		

DAY	TIME		SERVICE	CUSTOMER
MONTH .... **YEAR**	**8** AM	00		
		30		
TO DO LIST	**9** AM	00		
		30		
	10 AM	00		
		30		
	11 AM	00		
		30		
	12 PM	00		
MATERIALS LIST		30		
	1 PM	00		
		30		
	2 PM	00		
		30		
	3 PM	00		
		30		
QUOTES	**4** PM	00		
		30		
	5 PM	00		
		30		
	6 PM	00		
		30		
	7 PM	00		
		30		
	8 PM	00		
		30		

DAY	TIME		SERVICE	CUSTOMER
MONTH .... **YEAR**	**8** AM	00		
		30		
TO DO LIST	**9** AM	00		
		30		
	10 AM	00		
		30		
	11 AM	00		
		30		
	12 PM	00		
MATERIALS LIST		30		
	1 PM	00		
		30		
	2 PM	00		
		30		
	3 PM	00		
		30		
QUOTES	**4** PM	00		
		30		
	5 PM	00		
		30		
	6 PM	00		
		30		
	7 PM	00		
		30		
	8 PM	00		
		30		

DAY MONTH .... YEAR	TIME		SERVICE	CUSTOMER
TO DO LIST	8 AM	00		
		30		
	9 AM	00		
		30		
	10 AM	00		
		30		
	11 AM	00		
		30		
	12 PM	00		
MATERIALS LIST		30		
	1 PM	00		
		30		
	2 PM	00		
		30		
	3 PM	00		
		30		
QUOTES	4 PM	00		
		30		
	5 PM	00		
		30		
	6 PM	00		
		30		
	7 PM	00		
		30		
	8 PM	00		
		30		

DAY	TIME		SERVICE	CUSTOMER
MONTH .... **YEAR**	**8** AM	00		
		30		
TO DO LIST	**9** AM	00		
		30		
	10 AM	00		
		30		
	11 AM	00		
		30		
	12 PM	00		
MATERIALS LIST		30		
	1 PM	00		
		30		
	2 PM	00		
		30		
	3 PM	00		
		30		
QUOTES	**4** PM	00		
		30		
	5 PM	00		
		30		
	6 PM	00		
		30		
	7 PM	00		
		30		
	8 PM	00		
		30		

DAY	TIME		SERVICE	CUSTOMER
MONTH .... **YEAR**	**8** AM	00		
		30		
TO DO LIST	**9** AM	00		
		30		
	10 AM	00		
		30		
	11 AM	00		
		30		
	12 PM	00		
MATERIALS LIST		30		
	1 PM	00		
		30		
	2 PM	00		
		30		
	3 PM	00		
		30		
QUOTES	**4** PM	00		
		30		
	5 PM	00		
		30		
	6 PM	00		
		30		
	7 PM	00		
		30		
	8 PM	00		
		30		

SCHEDULE ▼ APPOINTMENTS ▼ PLANNER

DAY	TIME		SERVICE	CUSTOMER
MONTH .... **YEAR**	8 AM	00		
		30		
TO DO LIST	9 AM	00		
		30		
	10 AM	00		
		30		
	11 AM	00		
		30		
	12 PM	00		
MATERIALS LIST		30		
	1 PM	00		
		30		
	2 PM	00		
		30		
	3 PM	00		
		30		
QUOTES	4 PM	00		
		30		
	5 PM	00		
		30		
	6 PM	00		
		30		
	7 PM	00		
		30		
	8 PM	00		
		30		

DAY		TIME		SERVICE	CUSTOMER
MONTH		**8** AM	00		
YEAR			30		
TO DO LIST		**9** AM	00		
			30		
		10 AM	00		
			30		
		11 AM	00		
			30		
		12 PM	00		
MATERIALS LIST			30		
		1 PM	00		
			30		
		2 PM	00		
			30		
		3 PM	00		
			30		
QUOTES		**4** PM	00		
			30		
		5 PM	00		
			30		
		6 PM	00		
			30		
		7 PM	00		
			30		
		8 PM	00		
			30		

			TIME		SERVICE	CUSTOMER
DAY			**8** AM	00		
MONTH	....			30		
YEAR	....		**9** AM	00		
TO DO LIST				30		
			10 AM	00		
				30		
			11 AM	00		
				30		
			12 PM	00		
MATERIALS LIST				30		
			1 PM	00		
				30		
			2 PM	00		
				30		
			3 PM	00		
				30		
QUOTES			**4** PM	00		
				30		
			5 PM	00		
				30		
			6 PM	00		
				30		
			7 PM	00		
				30		
			8 PM	00		
				30		

SCHEDULE ▼ APPOINTMENTS ▼ PLANNER

DAY	TIME		SERVICE	CUSTOMER
MONTH .... **YEAR**	**8** AM	00		
		30		
TO DO LIST	**9** AM	00		
		30		
	10 AM	00		
		30		
	11 AM	00		
		30		
	12 PM	00		
MATERIALS LIST		30		
	1 PM	00		
		30		
	2 PM	00		
		30		
	3 PM	00		
		30		
QUOTES	**4** PM	00		
		30		
	5 PM	00		
		30		
	6 PM	00		
		30		
	7 PM	00		
		30		
	8 PM	00		
		30		

DAY MONTH .... YEAR	TIME		SERVICE	CUSTOMER
	8 AM	00		
		30		
TO DO LIST	9 AM	00		
		30		
	10 AM	00		
		30		
	11 AM	00		
		30		
	12 PM	00		
MATERIALS LIST		30		
	1 PM	00		
		30		
	2 PM	00		
		30		
	3 PM	00		
		30		
QUOTES	4 PM	00		
		30		
	5 PM	00		
		30		
	6 PM	00		
		30		
	7 PM	00		
		30		
	8 PM	00		
		30		

DAY		TIME		SERVICE	CUSTOMER
DAY MONTH .... YEAR		8 AM	00		
			30		
TO DO LIST		9 AM	00		
			30		
		10 AM	00		
			30		
		11 AM	00		
			30		
		12 PM	00		
MATERIALS LIST			30		
		1 PM	00		
			30		
		2 PM	00		
			30		
		3 PM	00		
			30		
QUOTES		4 PM	00		
			30		
		5 PM	00		
			30		
		6 PM	00		
			30		
		7 PM	00		
			30		
		8 PM	00		
			30		

DAY	TIME		SERVICE	CUSTOMER
MONTH	8 AM	00		
YEAR		30		
TO DO LIST	9 AM	00		
		30		
	10 AM	00		
		30		
	11 AM	00		
		30		
	12 PM	00		
MATERIALS LIST		30		
	1 PM	00		
		30		
	2 PM	00		
		30		
	3 PM	00		
		30		
QUOTES	4 PM	00		
		30		
	5 PM	00		
		30		
	6 PM	00		
		30		
	7 PM	00		
		30		
	8 PM	00		
		30		

DAY	TIME		SERVICE	CUSTOMER
MONTH .... **YEAR**	**8** AM	00		
		30		
TO DO LIST	**9** AM	00		
		30		
	10 AM	00		
		30		
	11 AM	00		
		30		
	12 PM	00		
MATERIALS LIST		30		
	1 PM	00		
		30		
	2 PM	00		
		30		
	3 PM	00		
		30		
QUOTES	**4** PM	00		
		30		
	5 PM	00		
		30		
	6 PM	00		
		30		
	7 PM	00		
		30		
	8 PM	00		
		30		

SCHEDULE ▼ APPOINTMENTS ▼ PLANNER

	TIME		SERVICE	CUSTOMER
DAY .... MONTH .... YEAR	8 AM	00		
		30		
TO DO LIST	9 AM	00		
		30		
	10 AM	00		
		30		
	11 AM	00		
		30		
	12 PM	00		
MATERIALS LIST		30		
	1 PM	00		
		30		
	2 PM	00		
		30		
	3 PM	00		
		30		
QUOTES	4 PM	00		
		30		
	5 PM	00		
		30		
	6 PM	00		
		30		
	7 PM	00		
		30		
	8 PM	00		
		30		

DAY	TIME		SERVICE	CUSTOMER
MONTH .... **YEAR**	**8** AM	00		
		30		
TO DO LIST	**9** AM	00		
		30		
	10 AM	00		
		30		
	11 AM	00		
		30		
	12 PM	00		
MATERIALS LIST		30		
	1 PM	00		
		30		
	2 PM	00		
		30		
	3 PM	00		
		30		
QUOTES	**4** PM	00		
		30		
	5 PM	00		
		30		
	6 PM	00		
		30		
	7 PM	00		
		30		
	8 PM	00		
		30		

DAY				TIME		SERVICE	CUSTOMER
MONTH				**8** AM	00		
YEAR					30		
TO DO LIST				**9** AM	00		
					30		
				10 AM	00		
					30		
				11 AM	00		
					30		
				12 PM	00		
MATERIALS LIST					30		
				1 PM	00		
					30		
				2 PM	00		
					30		
				3 PM	00		
					30		
QUOTES				**4** PM	00		
					30		
				5 PM	00		
					30		
				6 PM	00		
					30		
				7 PM	00		
					30		
				8 PM	00		
					30		

SCHEDULE ▼ APPOINTMENTS ▼ PLANNER

DAY .... MONTH .... YEAR	TIME		SERVICE	CUSTOMER
	8 AM	00		
		30		
TO DO LIST	9 AM	00		
		30		
	10 AM	00		
		30		
	11 AM	00		
		30		
	12 PM	00		
MATERIALS LIST		30		
	1 PM	00		
		30		
	2 PM	00		
		30		
	3 PM	00		
		30		
QUOTES	4 PM	00		
		30		
	5 PM	00		
		30		
	6 PM	00		
		30		
	7 PM	00		
		30		
	8 PM	00		
		30		

DAY			TIME		SERVICE	CUSTOMER
MONTH			**8** AM	00		
YEAR				30		
TO DO LIST			**9** AM	00		
				30		
			10 AM	00		
				30		
			11 AM	00		
				30		
			12 PM	00		
MATERIALS LIST				30		
			1 PM	00		
				30		
			2 PM	00		
				30		
			3 PM	00		
				30		
QUOTES			**4** PM	00		
				30		
			5 PM	00		
				30		
			6 PM	00		
				30		
			7 PM	00		
				30		
			8 PM	00		
				30		

DAY	TIME		SERVICE	CUSTOMER
MONTH	**8** AM	00		
YEAR		30		
TO DO LIST	**9** AM	00		
		30		
	10 AM	00		
		30		
	11 AM	00		
		30		
	12 PM	00		
MATERIALS LIST		30		
	1 PM	00		
		30		
	2 PM	00		
		30		
	3 PM	00		
		30		
QUOTES	**4** PM	00		
		30		
	5 PM	00		
		30		
	6 PM	00		
		30		
	7 PM	00		
		30		
	8 PM	00		
		30		

DAY		TIME		SERVICE	CUSTOMER
MONTH .... YEAR		8 AM	00		
			30		
TO DO LIST		9 AM	00		
			30		
		10 AM	00		
			30		
		11 AM	00		
			30		
		12 PM	00		
MATERIALS LIST			30		
		1 PM	00		
			30		
		2 PM	00		
			30		
		3 PM	00		
			30		
QUOTES		4 PM	00		
			30		
		5 PM	00		
			30		
		6 PM	00		
			30		
		7 PM	00		
			30		
		8 PM	00		
			30		

SCHEDULE ▼ APPOINTMENTS ▼ PLANNER

DAY	TIME		SERVICE	CUSTOMER
MONTH .... YEAR	8 AM	00		
		30		
TO DO LIST	9 AM	00		
		30		
	10 AM	00		
		30		
	11 AM	00		
		30		
	12 PM	00		
MATERIALS LIST		30		
	1 PM	00		
		30		
	2 PM	00		
		30		
	3 PM	00		
		30		
QUOTES	4 PM	00		
		30		
	5 PM	00		
		30		
	6 PM	00		
		30		
	7 PM	00		
		30		
	8 PM	00		
		30		

DAY _____ MONTH ·········· YEAR ··········	TIME		SERVICE	CUSTOMER
	8 AM	00		
		30		
TO DO LIST	**9** AM	00		
		30		
	10 AM	00		
		30		
	11 AM	00		
		30		
	12 PM	00		
MATERIALS LIST		30		
	1 PM	00		
		30		
	2 PM	00		
		30		
	3 PM	00		
		30		
QUOTES	**4** PM	00		
		30		
	5 PM	00		
		30		
	6 PM	00		
		30		
	7 PM	00		
		30		
	8 PM	00		
		30		

DAY	TIME		SERVICE	CUSTOMER
MONTH .... **YEAR**	8 AM	00		
		30		
TO DO LIST	9 AM	00		
		30		
	10 AM	00		
		30		
	11 AM	00		
		30		
	12 PM	00		
MATERIALS LIST		30		
	1 PM	00		
		30		
	2 PM	00		
		30		
	3 PM	00		
		30		
QUOTES	4 PM	00		
		30		
	5 PM	00		
		30		
	6 PM	00		
		30		
	7 PM	00		
		30		
	8 PM	00		
		30		

SCHEDULE ▼ APPOINTMENTS ▼ PLANNER

DAY .... MONTH .... YEAR	TIME		SERVICE	CUSTOMER
	8 AM	00		
		30		
TO DO LIST	**9** AM	00		
		30		
	10 AM	00		
		30		
	11 AM	00		
		30		
	12 PM	00		
MATERIALS LIST		30		
	1 PM	00		
		30		
	2 PM	00		
		30		
	3 PM	00		
		30		
QUOTES	**4** PM	00		
		30		
	5 PM	00		
		30		
	6 PM	00		
		30		
	7 PM	00		
		30		
	8 PM	00		
		30		

DAY MONTH .... YEAR	TIME		SERVICE	CUSTOMER
	8 AM	00		
		30		
TO DO LIST	**9** AM	00		
		30		
	10 AM	00		
		30		
	11 AM	00		
		30		
	12 PM	00		
MATERIALS LIST		30		
	1 PM	00		
		30		
	2 PM	00		
		30		
	3 PM	00		
		30		
QUOTES	**4** PM	00		
		30		
	5 PM	00		
		30		
	6 PM	00		
		30		
	7 PM	00		
		30		
	8 PM	00		
		30		

DAY		TIME		SERVICE	CUSTOMER
DAY		**8** AM	00		
MONTH			30		
YEAR		**9** AM	00		
TO DO LIST			30		
		10 AM	00		
			30		
		11 AM	00		
			30		
		12 PM	00		
MATERIALS LIST			30		
		1 PM	00		
			30		
		2 PM	00		
			30		
		3 PM	00		
			30		
QUOTES		**4** PM	00		
			30		
		5 PM	00		
			30		
		6 PM	00		
			30		
		7 PM	00		
			30		
		8 PM	00		
			30		

DAY	TIME		SERVICE	CUSTOMER
MONTH .... **YEAR**	**8** AM	00		
		30		
TO DO LIST	**9** AM	00		
		30		
	10 AM	00		
		30		
	11 AM	00		
		30		
	12 PM	00		
MATERIALS LIST		30		
	1 PM	00		
		30		
	2 PM	00		
		30		
	3 PM	00		
		30		
QUOTES	**4** PM	00		
		30		
	5 PM	00		
		30		
	6 PM	00		
		30		
	7 PM	00		
		30		
	8 PM	00		
		30		

DAY	**TIME**		**SERVICE**	**CUSTOMER**
MONTH .... **YEAR**	**8** AM	00		
		30		
TO DO LIST	**9** AM	00		
		30		
	10 AM	00		
		30		
	11 AM	00		
		30		
	12 PM	00		
MATERIALS LIST		30		
	1 PM	00		
		30		
	2 PM	00		
		30		
	3 PM	00		
		30		
QUOTES	**4** PM	00		
		30		
	5 PM	00		
		30		
	6 PM	00		
		30		
	7 PM	00		
		30		
	8 PM	00		
		30		

DAY					
MONTH					
YEAR					

	TIME		SERVICE	CUSTOMER
DAY MONTH .... YEAR	8 AM	00		
		30		
TO DO LIST	9 AM	00		
		30		
	10 AM	00		
		30		
	11 AM	00		
		30		
	12 PM	00		
MATERIALS LIST		30		
	1 PM	00		
		30		
	2 PM	00		
		30		
	3 PM	00		
		30		
QUOTES	4 PM	00		
		30		
	5 PM	00		
		30		
	6 PM	00		
		30		
	7 PM	00		
		30		
	8 PM	00		
		30		

DAY		TIME		SERVICE	CUSTOMER
MONTH		**8** AM	00		
YEAR			30		
TO DO LIST		**9** AM	00		
			30		
		10 AM	00		
			30		
		11 AM	00		
			30		
		12 PM	00		
MATERIALS LIST			30		
		1 PM	00		
			30		
		2 PM	00		
			30		
		3 PM	00		
			30		
QUOTES		**4** PM	00		
			30		
		5 PM	00		
			30		
		6 PM	00		
			30		
		7 PM	00		
			30		
		8 PM	00		
			30		

DAY	TIME		SERVICE	CUSTOMER
MONTH .... **YEAR**	8 AM	00		
		30		
TO DO LIST	9 AM	00		
		30		
	10 AM	00		
		30		
	11 AM	00		
		30		
	12 PM	00		
MATERIALS LIST		30		
	1 PM	00		
		30		
	2 PM	00		
		30		
	3 PM	00		
		30		
QUOTES	4 PM	00		
		30		
	5 PM	00		
		30		
	6 PM	00		
		30		
	7 PM	00		
		30		
	8 PM	00		
		30		

TIME		SERVICE	CUSTOMER

DAY
MONTH ....
YEAR ....

	8 AM	00		
		30		

TO DO LIST

	9 AM	00		
		30		
	10 AM	00		
		30		
	11 AM	00		
		30		
	12 PM	00		

MATERIALS LIST

	12 PM	30		
	1 PM	00		
		30		
	2 PM	00		
		30		
	3 PM	00		
		30		

QUOTES

	4 PM	00		
		30		
	5 PM	00		
		30		
	6 PM	00		
		30		
	7 PM	00		
		30		
	8 PM	00		
		30		

DAY					

DAY
MONTH ....
YEAR ....

TIME		SERVICE	CUSTOMER
8 AM	00		
	30		
9 AM	00		
	30		
10 AM	00		
	30		
11 AM	00		
	30		
12 PM	00		
	30		
1 PM	00		
	30		
2 PM	00		
	30		
3 PM	00		
	30		
4 PM	00		
	30		
5 PM	00		
	30		
6 PM	00		
	30		
7 PM	00		
	30		
8 PM	00		
	30		

TO DO LIST

MATERIALS LIST

QUOTES

DAY	TIME		SERVICE	CUSTOMER
MONTH .... **YEAR**	**8** AM	00		
		30		
TO DO LIST	**9** AM	00		
		30		
	10 AM	00		
		30		
	11 AM	00		
		30		
	12 PM	00		
MATERIALS LIST		30		
	1 PM	00		
		30		
	2 PM	00		
		30		
	3 PM	00		
		30		
QUOTES	**4** PM	00		
		30		
	5 PM	00		
		30		
	6 PM	00		
		30		
	7 PM	00		
		30		
	8 PM	00		
		30		

DAY	TIME		SERVICE	CUSTOMER
MONTH .... **YEAR**	8 AM	00		
		30		
TO DO LIST	9 AM	00		
		30		
	10 AM	00		
		30		
	11 AM	00		
		30		
	12 PM	00		
MATERIALS LIST		30		
	1 PM	00		
		30		
	2 PM	00		
		30		
	3 PM	00		
		30		
QUOTES	4 PM	00		
		30		
	5 PM	00		
		30		
	6 PM	00		
		30		
	7 PM	00		
		30		
	8 PM	00		
		30		

DAY			TIME		SERVICE	CUSTOMER
MONTH			**8** AM	00		
YEAR				30		
TO DO LIST			**9** AM	00		
				30		
			10 AM	00		
				30		
			11 AM	00		
				30		
			12 PM	00		
MATERIALS LIST				30		
			1 PM	00		
				30		
			2 PM	00		
				30		
			3 PM	00		
				30		
QUOTES			**4** PM	00		
				30		
			5 PM	00		
				30		
			6 PM	00		
				30		
			7 PM	00		
				30		
			8 PM	00		
				30		

DAY	TIME		SERVICE	CUSTOMER
MONTH .... YEAR	8 AM	00		
		30		
TO DO LIST	9 AM	00		
		30		
	10 AM	00		
		30		
	11 AM	00		
		30		
	12 PM	00		
MATERIALS LIST		30		
	1 PM	00		
		30		
	2 PM	00		
		30		
	3 PM	00		
		30		
QUOTES	4 PM	00		
		30		
	5 PM	00		
		30		
	6 PM	00		
		30		
	7 PM	00		
		30		
	8 PM	00		
		30		

DAY	TIME		SERVICE	CUSTOMER
MONTH .... **YEAR**	8 AM	00		
		30		
TO DO LIST	9 AM	00		
		30		
	10 AM	00		
		30		
	11 AM	00		
		30		
	12 PM	00		
MATERIALS LIST		30		
	1 PM	00		
		30		
	2 PM	00		
		30		
	3 PM	00		
		30		
QUOTES	4 PM	00		
		30		
	5 PM	00		
		30		
	6 PM	00		
		30		
	7 PM	00		
		30		
	8 PM	00		
		30		

DAY	TIME		SERVICE	CUSTOMER
MONTH .... **YEAR**	**8** AM	00		
		30		
TO DO LIST	**9** AM	00		
		30		
	10 AM	00		
		30		
	11 AM	00		
		30		
	12 PM	00		
MATERIALS LIST		30		
	1 PM	00		
		30		
	2 PM	00		
		30		
	3 PM	00		
		30		
QUOTES	**4** PM	00		
		30		
	5 PM	00		
		30		
	6 PM	00		
		30		
	7 PM	00		
		30		
	8 PM	00		
		30		

SCHEDULE ▼ APPOINTMENTS ▼ PLANNER

DAY MONTH YEAR	TIME		SERVICE	CUSTOMER
DAY	**8** AM	00		
MONTH		30		
YEAR	**9** AM	00		
		30		
TO DO LIST	**10** AM	00		
		30		
	11 AM	00		
		30		
	12 PM	00		
MATERIALS LIST		30		
	1 PM	00		
		30		
	2 PM	00		
		30		
	3 PM	00		
		30		
QUOTES	**4** PM	00		
		30		
	5 PM	00		
		30		
	6 PM	00		
		30		
	7 PM	00		
		30		
	8 PM	00		
		30		

DAY		TIME		SERVICE	CUSTOMER
MONTH		**8** AM	**00**		
YEAR			**30**		
TO DO LIST		**9** AM	**00**		
			30		
		10 AM	**00**		
			30		
		11 AM	**00**		
			30		
		12 PM	**00**		
MATERIALS LIST			**30**		
		1 PM	**00**		
			30		
		2 PM	**00**		
			30		
		3 PM	**00**		
			30		
QUOTES		**4** PM	**00**		
			30		
		5 PM	**00**		
			30		
		6 PM	**00**		
			30		
		7 PM	**00**		
			30		
		8 PM	**00**		
			30		

DAY		TIME		SERVICE	CUSTOMER
MONTH .... **YEAR**		**8** AM	00		
			30		
TO DO LIST		**9** AM	00		
			30		
		10 AM	00		
			30		
		11 AM	00		
			30		
		12 PM	00		
MATERIALS LIST			30		
		1 PM	00		
			30		
		2 PM	00		
			30		
		3 PM	00		
			30		
QUOTES		**4** PM	00		
			30		
		5 PM	00		
			30		
		6 PM	00		
			30		
		7 PM	00		
			30		
		8 PM	00		
			30		

DAY		TIME		SERVICE	CUSTOMER
MONTH		**8** AM	00		
YEAR			30		
TO DO LIST		**9** AM	00		
			30		
		10 AM	00		
			30		
		11 AM	00		
			30		
		12 PM	00		
MATERIALS LIST			30		
		1 PM	00		
			30		
		2 PM	00		
			30		
		3 PM	00		
			30		
QUOTES		**4** PM	00		
			30		
		5 PM	00		
			30		
		6 PM	00		
			30		
		7 PM	00		
			30		
		8 PM	00		
			30		

SCHEDULE ▼ APPOINTMENTS ▼ PLANNER

DAY	TIME		SERVICE	CUSTOMER
MONTH .... **YEAR**	8 AM	00		
		30		
TO DO LIST	9 AM	00		
		30		
	10 AM	00		
		30		
	11 AM	00		
		30		
	12 PM	00		
MATERIALS LIST		30		
	1 PM	00		
		30		
	2 PM	00		
		30		
	3 PM	00		
		30		
QUOTES	4 PM	00		
		30		
	5 PM	00		
		30		
	6 PM	00		
		30		
	7 PM	00		
		30		
	8 PM	00		
		30		

SCHEDULE ▼ APPOINTMENTS ▼ PLANNER

DAY			TIME		SERVICE	CUSTOMER
MONTH			**8** AM	00		
YEAR				30		

DAY
MONTH
YEAR

TO DO LIST

MATERIALS LIST

QUOTES

TIME		SERVICE	CUSTOMER
8 AM	00		
	30		
9 AM	00		
	30		
10 AM	00		
	30		
11 AM	00		
	30		
12 PM	00		
	30		
1 PM	00		
	30		
2 PM	00		
	30		
3 PM	00		
	30		
4 PM	00		
	30		
5 PM	00		
	30		
6 PM	00		
	30		
7 PM	00		
	30		
8 PM	00		
	30		

DAY	TIME		SERVICE	CUSTOMER
MONTH .... **YEAR**	8 AM	00		
		30		
TO DO LIST	9 AM	00		
		30		
	10 AM	00		
		30		
	11 AM	00		
		30		
	12 PM	00		
MATERIALS LIST		30		
	1 PM	00		
		30		
	2 PM	00		
		30		
	3 PM	00		
		30		
QUOTES	4 PM	00		
		30		
	5 PM	00		
		30		
	6 PM	00		
		30		
	7 PM	00		
		30		
	8 PM	00		
		30		

SCHEDULE ▼ APPOINTMENTS ▼ PLANNER

DAY	TIME		SERVICE	CUSTOMER
MONTH .... **YEAR**	**8 AM**	00		
		30		
TO DO LIST	**9 AM**	00		
		30		
	10 AM	00		
		30		
	11 AM	00		
		30		
	12 PM	00		
MATERIALS LIST		30		
	1 PM	00		
		30		
	2 PM	00		
		30		
	3 PM	00		
		30		
QUOTES	**4 PM**	00		
		30		
	5 PM	00		
		30		
	6 PM	00		
		30		
	7 PM	00		
		30		
	8 PM	00		
		30		

DAY	TIME		SERVICE	CUSTOMER
MONTH	**8** AM	00		
YEAR		30		
TO DO LIST	**9** AM	00		
		30		
	10 AM	00		
		30		
	11 AM	00		
		30		
	12 PM	00		
MATERIALS LIST		30		
	1 PM	00		
		30		
	2 PM	00		
		30		
	3 PM	00		
		30		
QUOTES	**4** PM	00		
		30		
	5 PM	00		
		30		
	6 PM	00		
		30		
	7 PM	00		
		30		
	8 PM	00		
		30		

DAY				
DAY **MONTH** **YEAR**	**TIME**		**SERVICE**	**CUSTOMER**

	TIME		SERVICE	CUSTOMER
DAY .... **MONTH** .... **YEAR**	**8 AM**	**00**		
		30		
TO DO LIST	**9 AM**	**00**		
		30		
	10 AM	**00**		
		30		
	11 AM	**00**		
		30		
	12 PM	**00**		
MATERIALS LIST		**30**		
	1 PM	**00**		
		30		
	2 PM	**00**		
		30		
	3 PM	**00**		
		30		
QUOTES	**4 PM**	**00**		
		30		
	5 PM	**00**		
		30		
	6 PM	**00**		
		30		
	7 PM	**00**		
		30		
	8 PM	**00**		
		30		

DAY MONTH .... YEAR	TIME		SERVICE	CUSTOMER
	8 AM	00		
		30		
TO DO LIST	9 AM	00		
		30		
	10 AM	00		
		30		
	11 AM	00		
		30		
	12 PM	00		
MATERIALS LIST		30		
	1 PM	00		
		30		
	2 PM	00		
		30		
	3 PM	00		
		30		
QUOTES	4 PM	00		
		30		
	5 PM	00		
		30		
	6 PM	00		
		30		
	7 PM	00		
		30		
	8 PM	00		
		30		

SCHEDULE ▼ APPOINTMENTS ▼ PLANNER

DAY	TIME		SERVICE	CUSTOMER
MONTH .... **YEAR**	**8 AM**	00		
		30		
TO DO LIST	**9 AM**	00		
		30		
	10 AM	00		
		30		
	11 AM	00		
		30		
	12 PM	00		
MATERIALS LIST		30		
	1 PM	00		
		30		
	2 PM	00		
		30		
	3 PM	00		
		30		
QUOTES	**4 PM**	00		
		30		
	5 PM	00		
		30		
	6 PM	00		
		30		
	7 PM	00		
		30		
	8 PM	00		
		30		

DAY	TIME		SERVICE	CUSTOMER
MONTH .... **YEAR**	**8** AM	00		
		30		
TO DO LIST	**9** AM	00		
		30		
	10 AM	00		
		30		
	11 AM	00		
		30		
	12 PM	00		
MATERIALS LIST		30		
	1 PM	00		
		30		
	2 PM	00		
		30		
	3 PM	00		
		30		
QUOTES	**4** PM	00		
		30		
	5 PM	00		
		30		
	6 PM	00		
		30		
	7 PM	00		
		30		
	8 PM	00		
		30		

DAY	TIME		SERVICE	CUSTOMER
MONTH .... **YEAR**	**8** AM	00		
		30		
TO DO LIST	**9** AM	00		
		30		
	10 AM	00		
		30		
	11 AM	00		
		30		
	12 PM	00		
MATERIALS LIST		30		
	1 PM	00		
		30		
	2 PM	00		
		30		
	3 PM	00		
		30		
QUOTES	**4** PM	00		
		30		
	5 PM	00		
		30		
	6 PM	00		
		30		
	7 PM	00		
		30		
	8 PM	00		
		30		

DAY			TIME		SERVICE	CUSTOMER
MONTH			8 AM	00		
YEAR				30		
TO DO LIST			9 AM	00		
				30		
			10 AM	00		
				30		
			11 AM	00		
				30		
			12 PM	00		
MATERIALS LIST				30		
			1 PM	00		
				30		
			2 PM	00		
				30		
			3 PM	00		
				30		
QUOTES			4 PM	00		
				30		
			5 PM	00		
				30		
			6 PM	00		
				30		
			7 PM	00		
				30		
			8 PM	00		
				30		

DAY				
MONTH				
YEAR				

DAY
MONTH ....
YEAR ....

TIME		SERVICE	CUSTOMER
8 AM	00		
	30		
9 AM	00		
	30		
10 AM	00		
	30		
11 AM	00		
	30		
12 PM	00		
	30		
1 PM	00		
	30		
2 PM	00		
	30		
3 PM	00		
	30		
4 PM	00		
	30		
5 PM	00		
	30		
6 PM	00		
	30		
7 PM	00		
	30		
8 PM	00		
	30		

TO DO LIST

MATERIALS LIST

QUOTES

	TIME		SERVICE	CUSTOMER
DAY .... **MONTH** .... **YEAR**	**8** AM	00		
		30		
TO DO LIST	**9** AM	00		
		30		
	10 AM	00		
		30		
	11 AM	00		
		30		
	12 PM	00		
MATERIALS LIST		30		
	1 PM	00		
		30		
	2 PM	00		
		30		
	3 PM	00		
		30		
QUOTES	**4** PM	00		
		30		
	5 PM	00		
		30		
	6 PM	00		
		30		
	7 PM	00		
		30		
	8 PM	00		
		30		

	TIME		SERVICE	CUSTOMER
DAY .... **MONTH** .... **YEAR**	**8** AM	**00**		
		30		
TO DO LIST	**9** AM	**00**		
		30		
	10 AM	**00**		
		30		
	11 AM	**00**		
		30		
	12 PM	**00**		
MATERIALS LIST		**30**		
	1 PM	**00**		
		30		
	2 PM	**00**		
		30		
	3 PM	**00**		
		30		
QUOTES	**4** PM	**00**		
		30		
	5 PM	**00**		
		30		
	6 PM	**00**		
		30		
	7 PM	**00**		
		30		
	8 PM	**00**		
		30		

DAY		TIME		SERVICE	CUSTOMER
MONTH		8 AM	00		
YEAR			30		
TO DO LIST		9 AM	00		
			30		
		10 AM	00		
			30		
		11 AM	00		
			30		
		12 PM	00		
MATERIALS LIST			30		
		1 PM	00		
			30		
		2 PM	00		
			30		
		3 PM	00		
			30		
QUOTES		4 PM	00		
			30		
		5 PM	00		
			30		
		6 PM	00		
			30		
		7 PM	00		
			30		
		8 PM	00		
			30		

DAY					
DAY			**TIME**	**SERVICE**	**CUSTOMER**

	TIME		SERVICE	CUSTOMER
DAY **MONTH** .... **YEAR**	**8** AM	00		
		30		
TO DO LIST	**9** AM	00		
		30		
	10 AM	00		
		30		
	11 AM	00		
		30		
	12 PM	00		
MATERIALS LIST		30		
	1 PM	00		
		30		
	2 PM	00		
		30		
	3 PM	00		
		30		
QUOTES	**4** PM	00		
		30		
	5 PM	00		
		30		
	6 PM	00		
		30		
	7 PM	00		
		30		
	8 PM	00		
		30		

DAY	TIME		SERVICE	CUSTOMER
MONTH .... **YEAR**	**8** AM	00		
		30		
TO DO LIST	**9** AM	00		
		30		
	10 AM	00		
		30		
	11 AM	00		
		30		
	12 PM	00		
MATERIALS LIST		30		
	1 PM	00		
		30		
	2 PM	00		
		30		
	3 PM	00		
		30		
QUOTES	**4** PM	00		
		30		
	5 PM	00		
		30		
	6 PM	00		
		30		
	7 PM	00		
		30		
	8 PM	00		
		30		

DAY	TIME		SERVICE	CUSTOMER
MONTH .... **YEAR**	**8** AM	00		
		30		
TO DO LIST	**9** AM	00		
		30		
	10 AM	00		
		30		
	11 AM	00		
		30		
	12 PM	00		
MATERIALS LIST		30		
	1 PM	00		
		30		
	2 PM	00		
		30		
	3 PM	00		
		30		
QUOTES	**4** PM	00		
		30		
	5 PM	00		
		30		
	6 PM	00		
		30		
	7 PM	00		
		30		
	8 PM	00		
		30		

SCHEDULE ▼ APPOINTMENTS ▼ PLANNER

DAY	TIME		SERVICE	CUSTOMER
MONTH .... **YEAR**	**8** AM	00		
		30		
TO DO LIST	**9** AM	00		
		30		
	10 AM	00		
		30		
	11 AM	00		
		30		
	12 PM	00		
MATERIALS LIST		30		
	1 PM	00		
		30		
	2 PM	00		
		30		
	3 PM	00		
		30		
QUOTES	**4** PM	00		
		30		
	5 PM	00		
		30		
	6 PM	00		
		30		
	7 PM	00		
		30		
	8 PM	00		
		30		

DAY				
MONTH				
YEAR				

	TIME		SERVICE	CUSTOMER
DAY	**8** AM	00		
MONTH		30		
YEAR	**9** AM	00		
TO DO LIST		30		
	10 AM	00		
		30		
	11 AM	00		
		30		
	12 PM	00		
MATERIALS LIST		30		
	1 PM	00		
		30		
	2 PM	00		
		30		
	3 PM	00		
		30		
QUOTES	**4** PM	00		
		30		
	5 PM	00		
		30		
	6 PM	00		
		30		
	7 PM	00		
		30		
	8 PM	00		
		30		

	TIME		SERVICE	CUSTOMER
DAY	8 AM	00		
MONTH		30		
YEAR	9 AM	00		
TO DO LIST		30		
	10 AM	00		
		30		
	11 AM	00		
		30		
	12 PM	00		
MATERIALS LIST		30		
	1 PM	00		
		30		
	2 PM	00		
		30		
	3 PM	00		
		30		
QUOTES	4 PM	00		
		30		
	5 PM	00		
		30		
	6 PM	00		
		30		
	7 PM	00		
		30		
	8 PM	00		
		30		

DAY
MONTH ....
YEAR ....

TIME		SERVICE	CUSTOMER
8 AM	**00**		
	30		
9 AM	**00**		
	30		
10 AM	**00**		
	30		
11 AM	**00**		
	30		
12 PM	**00**		
	30		
1 PM	**00**		
	30		
2 PM	**00**		
	30		
3 PM	**00**		
	30		
4 PM	**00**		
	30		
5 PM	**00**		
	30		
6 PM	**00**		
	30		
7 PM	**00**		
	30		
8 PM	**00**		
	30		

TO DO LIST

MATERIALS LIST

QUOTES

DAY	TIME		SERVICE	CUSTOMER
MONTH .... **YEAR**	8 AM	00		
		30		
TO DO LIST	9 AM	00		
		30		
	10 AM	00		
		30		
	11 AM	00		
		30		
	12 PM	00		
MATERIALS LIST		30		
	1 PM	00		
		30		
	2 PM	00		
		30		
	3 PM	00		
		30		
QUOTES	4 PM	00		
		30		
	5 PM	00		
		30		
	6 PM	00		
		30		
	7 PM	00		
		30		
	8 PM	00		
		30		

DAY
MONTH ....
YEAR ....

TO DO LIST

MATERIALS LIST

QUOTES

TIME		SERVICE	CUSTOMER
8 AM	00		
	30		
9 AM	00		
	30		
10 AM	00		
	30		
11 AM	00		
	30		
12 PM	00		
	30		
1 PM	00		
	30		
2 PM	00		
	30		
3 PM	00		
	30		
4 PM	00		
	30		
5 PM	00		
	30		
6 PM	00		
	30		
7 PM	00		
	30		
8 PM	00		
	30		

DAY	TIME		SERVICE	CUSTOMER
MONTH .... **YEAR**	**8** AM	00		
		30		
TO DO LIST	**9** AM	00		
		30		
	10 AM	00		
		30		
	11 AM	00		
		30		
	12 PM	00		
MATERIALS LIST		30		
	1 PM	00		
		30		
	2 PM	00		
		30		
	3 PM	00		
		30		
QUOTES	**4** PM	00		
		30		
	5 PM	00		
		30		
	6 PM	00		
		30		
	7 PM	00		
		30		
	8 PM	00		
		30		

DAY	TIME		SERVICE	CUSTOMER
MONTH .... **YEAR**	**8** AM	00		
		30		
TO DO LIST	**9** AM	00		
		30		
	10 AM	00		
		30		
	11 AM	00		
		30		
	12 PM	00		
MATERIALS LIST		30		
	1 PM	00		
		30		
	2 PM	00		
		30		
	3 PM	00		
		30		
QUOTES	**4** PM	00		
		30		
	5 PM	00		
		30		
	6 PM	00		
		30		
	7 PM	00		
		30		
	8 PM	00		
		30		

DAY	TIME		SERVICE	CUSTOMER
MONTH .... YEAR	8 AM	00		
		30		
TO DO LIST	9 AM	00		
		30		
	10 AM	00		
		30		
	11 AM	00		
		30		
	12 PM	00		
MATERIALS LIST		30		
	1 PM	00		
		30		
	2 PM	00		
		30		
	3 PM	00		
		30		
QUOTES	4 PM	00		
		30		
	5 PM	00		
		30		
	6 PM	00		
		30		
	7 PM	00		
		30		
	8 PM	00		
		30		

DAY		TIME		SERVICE	CUSTOMER
MONTH		**8** AM	00		
YEAR			30		
TO DO LIST		**9** AM	00		
			30		
		10 AM	00		
			30		
		11 AM	00		
			30		
		12 PM	00		
MATERIALS LIST			30		
		1 PM	00		
			30		
		2 PM	00		
			30		
		3 PM	00		
			30		
QUOTES		**4** PM	00		
			30		
		5 PM	00		
			30		
		6 PM	00		
			30		
		7 PM	00		
			30		
		8 PM	00		
			30		

DAY	TIME		SERVICE	CUSTOMER
MONTH .... **YEAR**	**8** AM	00		
		30		
TO DO LIST	**9** AM	00		
		30		
	10 AM	00		
		30		
	11 AM	00		
		30		
	12 PM	00		
MATERIALS LIST		30		
	1 PM	00		
		30		
	2 PM	00		
		30		
	3 PM	00		
		30		
QUOTES	**4** PM	00		
		30		
	5 PM	00		
		30		
	6 PM	00		
		30		
	7 PM	00		
		30		
	8 PM	00		
		30		

DAY				
MONTH				
YEAR				

TIME		SERVICE	CUSTOMER
8 AM	00		
	30		
9 AM	00		
	30		
10 AM	00		
	30		
11 AM	00		
	30		
12 PM	00		
	30		
1 PM	00		
	30		
2 PM	00		
	30		
3 PM	00		
	30		
4 PM	00		
	30		
5 PM	00		
	30		
6 PM	00		
	30		
7 PM	00		
	30		
8 PM	00		
	30		

TO DO LIST

MATERIALS LIST

QUOTES

DAY	TIME		SERVICE	CUSTOMER
MONTH .... **YEAR**	**8** AM	00		
		30		
TO DO LIST	**9** AM	00		
		30		
	10 AM	00		
		30		
	11 AM	00		
		30		
	12 PM	00		
MATERIALS LIST		30		
	1 PM	00		
		30		
	2 PM	00		
		30		
	3 PM	00		
		30		
QUOTES	**4** PM	00		
		30		
	5 PM	00		
		30		
	6 PM	00		
		30		
	7 PM	00		
		30		
	8 PM	00		
		30		

DAY	TIME		SERVICE	CUSTOMER
MONTH .... **YEAR**	**8** AM	00		
		30		
TO DO LIST	**9** AM	00		
		30		
	10 AM	00		
		30		
	11 AM	00		
		30		
	12 PM	00		
MATERIALS LIST		30		
	1 PM	00		
		30		
	2 PM	00		
		30		
	3 PM	00		
		30		
QUOTES	**4** PM	00		
		30		
	5 PM	00		
		30		
	6 PM	00		
		30		
	7 PM	00		
		30		
	8 PM	00		
		30		

DAY			TIME		SERVICE	CUSTOMER
MONTH			**8** AM	00		
YEAR				30		
TO DO LIST			**9** AM	00		
				30		
			10 AM	00		
				30		
			11 AM	00		
				30		
			12 PM	00		
MATERIALS LIST				30		
			1 PM	00		
				30		
			2 PM	00		
				30		
			3 PM	00		
				30		
QUOTES			**4** PM	00		
				30		
			5 PM	00		
				30		
			6 PM	00		
				30		
			7 PM	00		
				30		
			8 PM	00		
				30		

DAY

MONTH ....

YEAR ....

TO DO LIST

MATERIALS LIST

QUOTES

TIME		SERVICE	CUSTOMER
8 AM	00		
	30		
9 AM	00		
	30		
10 AM	00		
	30		
11 AM	00		
	30		
12 PM	00		
	30		
1 PM	00		
	30		
2 PM	00		
	30		
3 PM	00		
	30		
4 PM	00		
	30		
5 PM	00		
	30		
6 PM	00		
	30		
7 PM	00		
	30		
8 PM	00		
	30		

DAY MONTH .... YEAR	TIME		SERVICE	CUSTOMER
	8 AM	00		
		30		
TO DO LIST	9 AM	00		
		30		
	10 AM	00		
		30		
	11 AM	00		
		30		
	12 PM	00		
MATERIALS LIST		30		
	1 PM	00		
		30		
	2 PM	00		
		30		
	3 PM	00		
		30		
QUOTES	4 PM	00		
		30		
	5 PM	00		
		30		
	6 PM	00		
		30		
	7 PM	00		
		30		
	8 PM	00		
		30		

	TIME		SERVICE	CUSTOMER
DAY .... **MONTH** .... **YEAR**	**8** **AM**	00		
		30		
TO DO LIST	**9** **AM**	00		
		30		
	10 **AM**	00		
		30		
	11 **AM**	00		
		30		
	12 **PM**	00		
MATERIALS LIST		30		
	1 **PM**	00		
		30		
	2 **PM**	00		
		30		
	3 **PM**	00		
		30		
QUOTES	**4** **PM**	00		
		30		
	5 **PM**	00		
		30		
	6 **PM**	00		
		30		
	7 **PM**	00		
		30		
	8 **PM**	00		
		30		

DAY				

DAY		**TIME**		**SERVICE**	**CUSTOMER**
MONTH		**8** AM	**00**		
YEAR			**30**		
TO DO LIST		**9** AM	**00**		
			30		
		10 AM	**00**		
			30		
		11 AM	**00**		
			30		
		12 PM	**00**		
MATERIALS LIST			**30**		
		1 PM	**00**		
			30		
		2 PM	**00**		
			30		
		3 PM	**00**		
			30		
QUOTES		**4** PM	**00**		
			30		
		5 PM	**00**		
			30		
		6 PM	**00**		
			30		
		7 PM	**00**		
			30		
		8 PM	**00**		
			30		

SCHEDULE ▼ APPOINTMENTS ▼ PLANNER

DAY		TIME		SERVICE	CUSTOMER
MONTH		**8** AM	00		
YEAR			30		
TO DO LIST		**9** AM	00		
			30		
		10 AM	00		
			30		
		11 AM	00		
			30		
		12 PM	00		
MATERIALS LIST			30		
		1 PM	00		
			30		
		2 PM	00		
			30		
		3 PM	00		
			30		
QUOTES		**4** PM	00		
			30		
		5 PM	00		
			30		
		6 PM	00		
			30		
		7 PM	00		
			30		
		8 PM	00		
			30		

DAY			TIME		SERVICE	CUSTOMER
MONTH			**8** AM	00		
YEAR				30		
TO DO LIST			**9** AM	00		
				30		
			10 AM	00		
				30		
			11 AM	00		
				30		
			12 PM	00		
MATERIALS LIST				30		
			1 PM	00		
				30		
			2 PM	00		
				30		
			3 PM	00		
				30		
QUOTES			**4** PM	00		
				30		
			5 PM	00		
				30		
			6 PM	00		
				30		
			7 PM	00		
				30		
			8 PM	00		
				30		

DAY		TIME		SERVICE	CUSTOMER
MONTH		**8** AM	00		
YEAR			30		
TO DO LIST		**9** AM	00		
			30		
		10 AM	00		
			30		
		11 AM	00		
			30		
		12 PM	00		
MATERIALS LIST			30		
		1 PM	00		
			30		
		2 PM	00		
			30		
		3 PM	00		
			30		
QUOTES		**4** PM	00		
			30		
		5 PM	00		
			30		
		6 PM	00		
			30		
		7 PM	00		
			30		
		8 PM	00		
			30		

DAY	TIME		SERVICE	CUSTOMER
DAY MONTH .... YEAR	8 AM	00		
		30		
TO DO LIST	9 AM	00		
		30		
	10 AM	00		
		30		
	11 AM	00		
		30		
	12 PM	00		
MATERIALS LIST		30		
	1 PM	00		
		30		
	2 PM	00		
		30		
	3 PM	00		
		30		
QUOTES	4 PM	00		
		30		
	5 PM	00		
		30		
	6 PM	00		
		30		
	7 PM	00		
		30		
	8 PM	00		
		30		

NOTES:

NOTES:

NOTES:

NOTES: